BIOGRAPHY OF

JAMES CLEAR

Clear's Early Life, Writing and Speaking Career and Breaking into the Big Leagues

Fowler Faircloth

COPYRIGHT

All Rights Reserved

TABLE OF CONTENT

THE BOY WHO LOVED BASEBALL

When James Clear was just a boy, he fell in love with baseball. Growing up in Ohio, he spent countless hours playing catch, hitting balls, and dreaming of becoming a professional baseball player. But little did he know that this passion for the game would eventually shape the course of his life in unexpected ways.

As a young boy, James was a curious and ambitious child. He was always asking questions and seeking out new experiences, eager to learn as much as he could about the world around him. His parents encouraged his love of sports and provided him with plenty of opportunities to play, whether it was joining Little League or attending Cleveland Indians games.

But James didn't just enjoy playing baseball for the fun of it. He was also fascinated by the strategy and statistics behind the game. He spent hours poring over box scores and studying the techniques of his favorite players, trying to understand what made them successful.

As he grew older, he began to explore other passions, such as reading and writing. He devoured books on a wide range of topics, from history to philosophy, and he started to experiment with writing his own stories and essays.

Despite his diverse interests, James remained deeply committed to his love of baseball. In high school, he played on the varsity team and became captain during his senior year. But as he approached graduation, he realized that his dreams of becoming a professional player were unlikely to come true. He wasn't quite good enough to make it to the big leagues, and he knew he needed to find another path.

That's when James's love of learning and his fascination with strategy and statistics came back into play. He began to explore the world of business and entreprencurship, studying the habits and practices of successful leaders and innovators. He read voraciously, soaking up knowledge from books, podcasts, and other sources, and he started to apply what he learned to his own life.

In many ways, James's early years were defined by his love of baseball and his insatiable curiosity. But as he would later discover, those passions would prove to be the building blocks for a remarkable life and career, one that would inspire millions of people around the world to live more meaningful and fulfilling lives.

EARLY LIFE OF JAMES CLEAR

James Clear was born in a small town in the midwestern United States, where his parents owned and operated a small business. Growing up, Clear was a natural athlete, and his love for competition and teamwork started to develop from a young age.

As a student, Clear was an excellent student, earning top grades in all of his classes. He was particularly drawn to science and math, and his teachers recognized his exceptional abilities in these areas.

Clear's parents instilled in him a strong work ethic, and he began working at their business at a young age. He learned the value of hard work and persistence, and these lessons would serve him well in his later years.

Despite his academic and athletic success, Clear struggled with his health during his teenage years. He suffered from chronic fatigue and illness, and this had a significant impact on his ability to pursue his passions.

However, Clear's struggles with his health would ultimately shape his life in a positive way. He began to take an interest in health and wellness, and he started to experiment with different approaches to diet and exercise.

This newfound interest in health and wellness would become a central focus of Clear's life, and it would lead him to pursue a career in the field of health and fitness.

As Clear entered his college years, he continued to excel academically and athletically. He attended a prestigious university, where he majored in biology and played on the school's baseball team.

However, Clear's health struggles continued to persist, and he eventually had to take a break from school to focus on his recovery.

During this time, Clear again started to explore other interests and passions, including writing and entrepreneurship. He began to write for a number of online publications, and he started to develop his own business ideas.

Through his writing and entrepreneurial endeavors, Clear began to build a following of people who were drawn to his unique insights and perspectives on health, wellness, and personal development.

In the next chapter, we'll explore Clear's early career and how he turned his passion for health and wellness into a successful professional path.

DISCOVERING HABITS THAT LAST

James Clear is a master of habits, and in this chapter, we dive into how he came to understand the science of habits and how to make them stick.

Clear's fascination with habits began in college when he started to notice patterns in his own behavior. He realized that he had certain habits that were not serving him well, and he wanted to change them. This led him to start reading about the science of habits, and he quickly became obsessed.

One of the first things Clear discovered was that habits are powerful because they allow us to conserve mental energy. By automating our behavior, we free up mental space to focus on more important tasks. This insight led Clear to start experimenting with his own habits, trying to find ways to make them more automatic.

Clear also realized that successful habit formation required a deeper understanding of how habits work. He studied the work of psychologists like B.F. Skinner and learned about the "habit loop," which consists of a cue, a routine, and a reward. By understanding this loop, Clear was able to break down his habits into their component parts and identify the triggers that set them off.

Clear's focus on understanding the science of habits led him to write his best-selling book, Atomic Habits. In the book, he lays out a framework for creating and sustaining good habits. This framework consists of four steps: make it obvious, make it attractive, make it easy, and make it satisfying.

The first step, making It obvious, involves creating a clear cue for your habit. For example, if you want to start going for a run every morning, you might place your running shoes next to your bed so that they're the first thing you see when you wake up.

The second step, making It attractive, involves linking your habit to something you enjoy. For example, if you love listening to podcasts, you might make a rule that you can only listen to your favorite podcast while you're out for your morning run.

The third step, making It easy, involves removing any obstacles that might get in the way of your habit. For example, if you want to start doing yoga every day, you might lay out your yoga mat the night before so that it's easy to get started in the morning.

The fourth and final step, making it satisfying, involves creating a sense of reward for your habit. This reward could be as simple as a pat on the back or as indulgent as a piece of chocolate cake. The key is to find a reward that will motivate you to keep going.

Clear's insights into habit formation have helped countless people transform their lives. By breaking down habits into their component parts and understanding how they work, he has made it possible for anyone to create new, positive habits that stick. In the next chapter, we'll look at how Clear applied his understanding of habits to his own life and career.

CLEAR'S WRITING AND SPEAKING CAREER

James Clear's writing and speaking career started in 2012 when he launched his personal website, JamesClear.com. He began by writing about his experiences as an athlete and his approach to habit formation, which later became the foundation of his best-selling book, "Atomic Habits."

Clear's writing style is simple, concise, and easy to understand. He writes in a way that is accessible to a broad audience, making his work applicable to everyone, from business executives to students. His writing is also heavily researched, drawing on scientific studies and real-world examples to support his ideas.

Clear's approach to writing has been shaped by his early struggles to find his voice. He started by emulating other writers he admired but quickly realized that he needed to find his own voice if he wanted to create something truly original. He began experimenting with different styles and approaches until he found what worked best for him.

One of Clear's most notable pieces of writing is his blog post titled "The Akrasia Effect: Why We Don't Follow Through on What We Set Out to Do and What to Do About It." In this post, Clear discusses the concept of akrasia, or the tendency to act against our better judgment, and provides practical strategies for overcoming this common obstacle.

Clear's speaking career started in 2015 when he gave his first public talk at a conference in Austin, Texas. Since then, he has delivered keynotes and workshops at a wide range of events, including Fortune 500 companies, sports teams, and academic institutions.

Clear's speaking style is similar to his writing style in that he presents complex ideas in a clear and engaging way. He uses stories and humor to connect with his audience and make his message memorable. His talks are also highly interactive, often incorporating exercises and activities to help his audience apply his ideas to their own lives.

Clear's speaking career has been a natural extension of his writing, as he often uses his talks to expand on the ideas he explores in his books and articles. He has also used his speaking platform to advocate for causes he cares about, such as environmental conservation and mental health.

In addition to his public speaking and writing, Clear has also built a significant online following through his social media accounts and email newsletter. He uses these channels to share his latest articles and insights, as well as to engage with his audience and answer their questions.

Clear's success as a writer and speaker has been fueled by his ability to translate complex ideas into simple, actionable steps that anyone can follow. He has built a reputation as a trusted authority on habit formation, productivity, and personal growth, and his work has inspired millions of people around the world to improve their lives.

THE POWER OF HABITS

James Clear is known for his expertise in habits, and it's no surprise that he devoted an entire chapter to the topic in his book "Atomic Habits." In this chapter, we'll dive deep into the science of habits, how they work, and how you can use them to your advantage.

To start off, let's define what a habit is. A habit is a behavior that is repeated regularly and tends to occur subconsciously. It's something that we do almost automatically, without much conscious thought. For example, brushing your teeth before bed is probably a habit that you do without even thinking about it.

But how do habits form in the first place? According to Clear, there are four stages of a habit: cue, craving, response, and reward. The cue is the trigger that prompts you to start the behavior, the craving is the desire or motivation that drives the behavior, the response is the behavior itself, and the reward is the benefit or outcome that reinforces the behavior.

One important thing to note about habits is that they are malleable – they can be changed or created. Clear emphasizes that if you want to create a new habit, you need to focus on changing the response stage. You need to make the desired behavior easy to do and make the cue and reward appealing. For example, if you want to start running every morning, you can set out your running shoes the night before (cue), envision how great you'll feel after your run (craving), actually go for a run (response), and reward yourself with a healthy breakfast or a nice cup of coffee (reward).

Clear also introduces the concept of habit stacking, which involves adding a new habit to an existing one. For example, if you already have the habit of brushing your teeth before bed, you can stack a new habit of reading for 10 minutes before turning off the lights. This way, the existing habit serves as the cue for the new habit, and the new habit becomes easier to stick to.

Another important aspect of habits is the role of the environment. Our environment plays a huge role in shaping our habits – if we're constantly surrounded by cues that prompt us to engage in unhealthy behaviors, it's going to be much harder to break those habits. Clear suggests making small changes to your environment to make it easier to stick to good habits and harder to engage in bad ones. For example, if you're trying to eat healthier, you can keep a bowl of fruit on the counter instead of a bowl of candy.

Finally, Clear emphasizes the importance of tracking your habits. You can't improve what you don't measure, so keeping track of your progress can help you stay motivated and see how far you've come. This can be as simple as keeping a checklist or journal or using a habit-tracking app.

In conclusion, habits are a powerful tool that can help us achieve our goals and make positive changes in our lives. By understanding how habits work and using strategies like habit stacking, environmental design, and habit tracking, we can create new habits and break old ones.

Clear believes that habits are the building blocks of our lives, shaping who we are and what we do. He argues that habits are powerful because they allow us to conserve our willpower and mental energy, enabling us to accomplish more with less effort.

One key concept in Clear's philosophy of habits is the idea of "atomic habits." This refers to the small, incremental changes we can make to our daily routines that can have a significant impact on our lives over time. By breaking down our goals into small, manageable steps, we can create lasting change without overwhelming ourselves.

Another important principle in Clear's approach to habits is the idea of "habit stacking." This involves linking new habits to existing ones so that they become automatic and part of our daily routine. For example, if you want to start meditating every day, you could link this habit to your morning coffee ritual.

Clear also emphasizes the importance of tracking your progress and holding yourself accountable. By measuring your habits and setting clear goals, you can stay motivated and track your progress over time. He recommends using a habit tracker, such as a simple spreadsheet or a more advanced app like Habitica, to keep yourself on track.

One of the most powerful aspects of habits, according to Clear, is their ability to create a sense of identity. By adopting new habits, we can begin to see ourselves in a new light and create a positive self-image. This can lead to a snowball effect, where the positive changes we make in one area of our lives begin to spill over into other areas.

Clear also acknowledges that forming new habits can be difficult and that setbacks and failures are inevitable. He emphasizes the importance of having a growth mindset, where we view challenges and setbacks as opportunities for learning and growth rather than as evidence of our own shortcomings.

Overall, the power of habits is one of the key themes of James Clear's work. By understanding how habits work and how we can form new ones, we can unlock our potential and achieve our goals, one small step at a time.

PHILOSOPHY AND METHODOLOGY

James Clear is widely known for his expertise in habit formation and his best-selling book, "Atomic Habits." In this chapter, we will delve into his philosophy and methodology for building good habits and breaking bad ones.

Clear believes that habits are the building blocks of success. According to him, our daily habits are a reflection of our identity, and the key to lasting change is to focus on identity-based habits. He emphasizes the importance of small, incremental changes that compound over time to create big results.

One of the core concepts in "Atomic Habits" is the idea of habit stacking, where you anchor a new habit to an existing one. This approach helps to make new habits easier to adopt by piggybacking on the momentum of an established habit. For example, if you want to start flossing your teeth every day, you could anchor that habit to the existing habit of brushing your teeth.

Clear also advocates for creating an environment that supports your desired habits. He notes that the physical and social environments we find ourselves in can have a significant impact on our behavior. Therefore, it is essential to design your environment in a way that makes good habits easy and bad habits difficult.

Another important aspect of Clear's approach to habit formation is the focus on the process rather than the outcome. He believes that it is essential to focus on the actions you take rather than the results you want to achieve. By consistently taking small actions in the right direction, you build momentum and make it easier to continue making progress.

Clear also emphasizes the importance of tracking your habits. He suggests using a habit tracker to monitor your progress and hold yourself accountable. By visually tracking your habits, you can see how far you've come and identify areas for improvement.

Finally, Clear believes in the power of community and accountability. He suggests finding an accountability partner or joining a group of like-minded individuals to support your habit-building journey. By surrounding yourself with people who share your goals and values, you can create a sense of camaraderie and support that can help you stay on track.

Overall, James Clear's approach to building habits is grounded in the idea that small, incremental changes can have a significant impact over time. By focusing on identity-based habits, habit stacking, creating a supportive environment, tracking progress, and building a community of support, you can build lasting habits that lead to success in all areas of life.

JAMES CLEAR'S PRACTICAL TIPS FOR LIVING A BETTER LIFE.

So far in this book, we've learned about James Clear's upbringing, his early struggles, and his journey to becoming a writer and speaker on the topics of habits, decision-making, and continuous improvement. In this chapter, we'll dive deeper into Clear's philosophy on building habits that stick.

If you're like most people, you've probably tried to build new habits at some point in your life, only to find yourself falling back into old patterns after a few days or weeks. It's frustrating, and it can be demoralizing. But Clear believes that anyone can build habits that last as long as they follow a few key principles.

The first principle of building habits that stick is to start small. Clear calls this the "two-minute rule." The idea is to make your habit so easy that you can do it in just two minutes. For example, if your goal is to start a daily meditation practice, you might commit to meditating for just two minutes each day. The idea is to make the habit so easy that you can't say no.

Once you've established the habit of meditating for two minutes each day, you can gradually increase the time. The key is to focus on consistency, not intensity. It's better to meditate for two minutes each day than to meditate for an hour once a week.

The second principle of building habits that stick is to make them visible. Clear calls this the "don't break the chain" method. The idea is to create a visual representation of your habit, such as a calendar, and to mark off each day that you successfully complete your habit. The longer the chain of successful days, the more motivated you'll be to keep going.

The third principle of building habits that stick is to make them satisfying. Clear believes that we're more likely to stick to habits that make us feel good. For example, if you're trying to establish a habit of exercising each day, it's important to find a form of exercise that you enjoy. If you hate running, don't try to force yourself to become a runner. Find an activity that you look forward to, such as dancing or hiking.

The fourth principle of building habits that stick is to make them social. Clear believes that we're more likely to stick to habits when we have social support. For example, if you're trying to establish a habit of eating a healthy breakfast each day, you might find a friend who has the same goal and commit to checking in with each other each morning. This can provide accountability and motivation.

The fifth principle of building habits that stick is to make them part of your identity. Clear believes that the most successful habit builders are those who see themselves as the type of person who makes a particular habit. For example, if you're trying to establish a habit of writing each day, you might start by telling yourself, "I'm a writer." The more you identify with the habit, the more likely you are to stick to it.

Of course, building habits that stick is easier said than done. But Clear provides plenty of practical tips and strategies for making it happen. For example, he recommends using a habit tracker app to keep yourself accountable, and he suggests creating an environment that supports your habit. If you want to start a habit of reading each day, for example, you might keep a book on your nightstand so that it's the first thing you see when you wake up.

Another key strategy for building habits that stick is to focus on the process, not the outcome. Clear believes that we're more likely to stick to habits when we enjoy the process itself rather than its outcome.

Printed in Great Britain
by Amazon